D0572646

FAR-OUT GUIDE
to the
SOLAR SYSTEM

FAR-OUT GUIDE TO
URANUS

Mary Kay Carson

Bailey Books
an imprint of
Enslow Publishers, Inc.
40 Industrial Road
Box 398
Berkeley Heights, NJ 07922
USA
http://www.enslow.com

For Doris Uhlman, in thanks for the contributions of her artistic talents.

Bailey Books, an imprint of Enslow Publishers, Inc.

Library of Congress Cataloging-in-Publication Data

Carson, Mary Kay.
    Far-out guide to uranus / Mary Kay Carson.
        p. cm. — (Far-out guide to the solar system)
    Includes bibliographical references and index.
    Summary: "Presents information about Uranus, including fast facts, history, and technology used to study the planet"—Provided by publisher.
    ISBN 978-0-7660-3185-2 (Library Ed.)
    ISBN 978-1-59845-188-7 (Paperback Ed.)
    1. Uranus (Planet)—Juvenile literature. 2. Solar system—Juvenile literature. I. Title.
    QB681.C37 2011
    523.47—dc22
                                        2008050040

Printed in China

052010 Leo Paper Group, Heshan City, Guangdong, China

10 9 8 7 6 5 4 3 2 1   *4357.7649   11/10*

To Our Readers: We have done our best to make sure all Internet Addresses in this book were active and appropriate when we went to press. However, the author and the publisher have no control over and assume no liability for the material available on those Internet sites or on other Web sites they may link to. Any comments or suggestions can be sent by e-mail to comments@enslow.com or to the address on the back cover.

Image Credits: Enslow Publishers, Inc., p. 6; Erich Karkoschka (University of Arizona) and NASA, p. 29; Heidi Hammel (MIT) and NASA, pp. 8, 20, 21; Laura Kinoshita, 38–39; Lawrence Sromovsky, University of Wisconsin-Madison/W. M. Keck Observatory, pp. 3, 42; Lunar and Planetary Institute, 11; NASA, p. 26; NASA, ESA, and A. Feild (STScI), pp. 32, 35; NASA, ESA, L. Sromovsky and P. Fry (University of Wisconsin), H. Hammel (Space Science Institute), and K. Rages (SETI Institute), p. 30; NASA, ESA, and M. Showalter (SETI Institute), p. 36; NASA/JPL, pp. 1, 4–5, 9, 10, 13, 15, 17, 22, 23, 25, 33; NASA/JPL/USGS, p. 19.

Cover Image: Lawrence Sromovsky, University of Wisconsin-Madison/W. M. Keck Observatory

CONTENTS

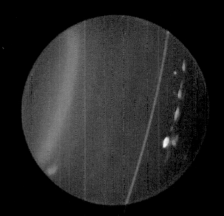

INTRODUCTION
4

CHAPTER 1
VOYAGER TO URANUS
9

URANUS AT A GLANCE
20

FAST FACTS ABOUT URANUS
21

URANUS TIMELINE OF
EXPLORATION AND DISCOVERY
24

CHAPTER 2
A TELESCOPIC VIEW
26

CHAPTER 3
WHAT'S NEXT FOR URANUS
38

WORDS TO KNOW
44

FIND OUT MORE
AND GET UPDATES
46

INDEX
48

URANUS is the seventh planet from the Sun. (Note that the planets' distances are not shown to scale.)

INTRODUCTION

William Herschel was not looking for a planet the night of March 13, 1781. The self-taught astronomer and telescope maker was tracking stars. When one looked fuzzy through his telescope, Herschel figured it was a comet. But after following the object's path for a few nights, Herschel realized he was wrong. The bright object was moving too slowly to be a comet. And its orbit was out past Saturn.

Hershel had instead found a seventh planet! It was the first planet ever discovered. People had been watching Mercury, Venus, Mars, Jupiter, and Saturn move across the night sky for thousands of years. Uranus was not identified as a planet until Herschel zoomed in on it with his newly built telescope.

STARS IN THE FAMILY

William Herschel (1738–1822) was a musician born in Germany. He moved to England as a young man. Years later, he read a book about telescopes and became interested in astronomy. He built some of the largest telescopes of his day and used them to discover hundreds of stars. William Herschel's sister Caroline Herschel (1750–1848) worked with him. She discovered eight comets and three nebulae. William's son and Caroline's nephew was John F. W. Herschel (1792–1871). He was also an important astronomer who discovered thousands of double stars, star clusters, and nebulae.

WILLIAM and Caroline Herschel observe the night sky. The large telescope is the one William was using in 1781 when he discovered Uranus. Six years later he used it to find two of Uranus's moons, Titania and Oberon.

A FASCINATING WORLD

Uranus is about twice as far from the Sun as Saturn is. Herschel's discovery of Uranus nearly doubled the known size of our solar system. Since then, astronomers have learned a lot about the seventh planet. Like Jupiter, Saturn, and Neptune, Uranus is a gas giant. It is a landless planet made of gases and liquids.

Uranus is a unique and fascinating place. It is the only one of our solar system's eight planets to be completely tilted over on its side. Instead of spinning like a top,

FAR-OUT FACT

NAME TROUBLE

William Herschel named the planet he discovered Georgium Sidus. It means "Georgian Planet" in Latin. The name was meant to honor England's King George III, who supported Herschel's work. In the early years following its discovery, many simply called the seventh planet "Herschel" instead. Neither name seemed to fit in very well with the mythological names of the other planets. So in 1850 the planet was officially named Uranus, after the Greek god of the heavens. It is pronounced YOOR-uh-nus.

Uranus turns like a bead on a string. No one knows why Uranus is sideways. Maybe something gigantic knocked it over millions of years ago. Uranus's sideways spin creates wacky seasons. Winter at Uranus's north pole is one long night that lasts for twenty-one years!

BECAUSE of Uranus's sideways tilt, sometimes one pole faces the Sun while the other points directly away from it.

CHAPTER 1

VOYAGER TO URANUS

Voyager 2 taught us much of what we know about Uranus. *Voyager 2* and its twin, *Voyager 1*, are robotic spacecraft, or space probes. *Voyager 2* left Earth atop a rocket in August 1977. *Voyager 1* launched two weeks later. *Voyager 1*'s main mission was visiting Jupiter, Saturn, and their moons. *Voyager 2* was a backup, in case something happened to *Voyager 1*.

Both Voyagers made it to Jupiter in 1979 without a problem. The sister space probes also success- fully visited Saturn two years later. *Voyager 1* then head- ed out of the solar system,

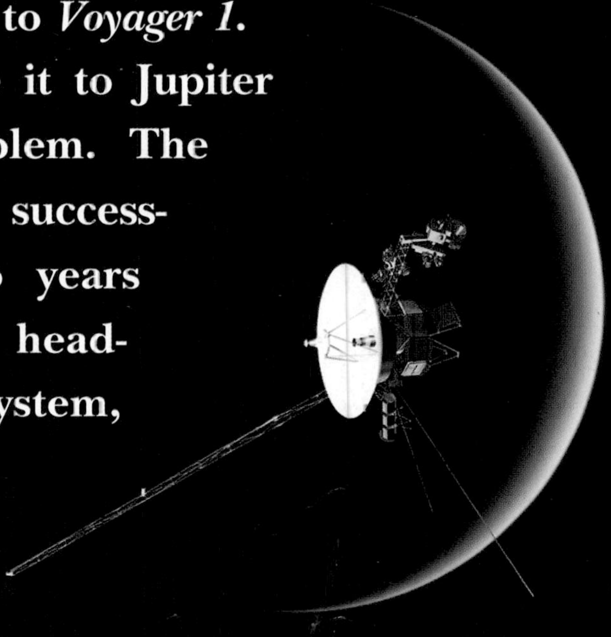

THIS illustration shows *Voyager 2*, the first—and so far only—space probe to study Uranus.

9

as planned. It was the backup spacecraft's chance at the big time! NASA sent *Voyager 2* off toward Uranus. It would be the first space probe ever to visit the seventh planet.

LONG-DISTANCE UPGRADE

Even after four years in space, *Voyager 2* was in good shape as it left Saturn behind. The cameras and scientific instruments on the car-sized probe worked fine. It had plenty of fuel, too. But Uranus is nearly twice as far away as Saturn.

VOYAGER 2 launches atop a rocket on August 20, 1977. It left from the NASA Kennedy Space Flight Center at Cape Canaveral, Florida.

WHERE ARE VOYAGER 1 & 2 NOW?

Voyager 2 went on to make another historic first visit: It arrived at Neptune in 1989. *Voyager 2* then headed out of the solar system, like its twin, *Voyager 1*. (*Voyager 1* is now the most distant human-made object in space.) Both Voyager spacecraft have now traveled to the edge of our solar system. They have reached the beginning of interstellar space. With luck, they will continue sending reports to scientists on Earth until around 2025.

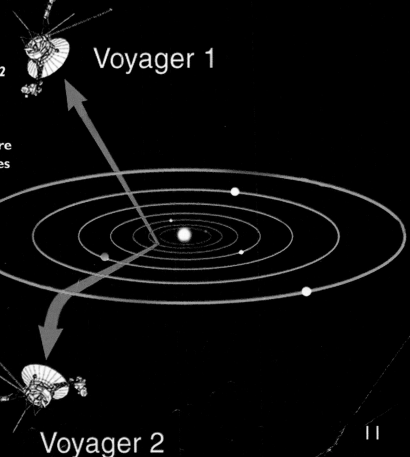

VOYAGER 1 and *Voyager 2* have left the solar system. In case someone out there finds the spacecraft, each carries a gold information disc. On it are messages, sounds, and pictures from Earth.

Voyager 1

Voyager 2

Voyager 2 was going to need to communicate with Earth from double the distance. Plus, Uranus only gets one-quarter of Saturn's sunlight. *Voyager 2* was going to have to take photographs in the near dark.

Voyager scientists and engineers quickly got to work. They needed to prepare their faraway spacecraft for its historic mission. On Earth, they improved the network of giant, dish-shaped antennas that receive information sent

FAR-OUT FACT

MEASURING A DAY

Astronomers measure the length of a planet's day by timing how long the planet takes to spin once. How? First they pick out a permanent feature on the planet, like a crater. Then they watch the planet spin, timing how long it takes for that feature to come back around. This is difficult to do with featureless planets, like Uranus. Before Voyager, astronomers could only guess. They thought a day on Uranus lasted between 15 and 24 hours. *Voyager 2* solved the mystery in 1986, timing Uranus's day at 17.24 hours.

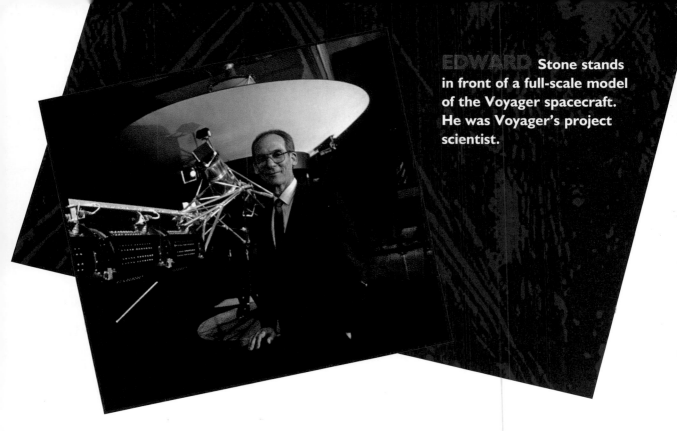

Stone stands in front of a full-scale model of the Voyager spacecraft. He was Voyager's project scientist.

by the Voyager spacecraft. Upgrading the spacecraft's computer software was another important job. Engineers uploaded new software to the space probe by radio signals. By the time it arrived at Uranus, *Voyager 2* was a smarter spacecraft.

ARRIVAL AT URANUS

"We've been waiting four and a half years for this," Edward Stone told reporters in early 1986. He had spent most of his career working on the Voyager project. Now he was in charge of Voyager's team of scientists and engineers. As *Voyager 2* neared Uranus, Stone knew

13

the view of the seventh planet was about to change. "It's going to be exciting," he said. "It has to be. We know so little."

On January 24, 1986, *Voyager 2* made its closest pass by Uranus. It came within 81,500 kilometers (50,600 miles) of the seventh planet's cloud tops. Traveling at 67,600 kilometers per hour (42,000 miles per hour), the space probe took thousands of pictures. Its eleven scientific instruments went to work measuring everything from wind speeds to Uranus's gravity. *Voyager 2* radioed its findings across 2.9 billion kilometers (1.8 billion miles) of space. Its signals took more than two and a half hours to reach Earth. Scientists watched as the information and images began arriving on their computers.

"I am happily bewildered," said Stone. "Uranus is just totally different than anything we have ever seen before."

Voyager 2 found Uranus's temperature oddly similar all over the planet. The pole facing away from the Sun was not any colder than the pole facing toward the Sun! *Voyager 2* measured winds of up to 580 kilometers per hour (360 miles per hour) on the seventh planet—faster than expected. Even more surprising were winds around Uranus's equator. *Voyager 2* discovered they blew in the opposite direction of the planet's spin at speeds of 355 kilometers per hour (220 miles per hour). That is twice as fast as Earth's jet stream. And there was a mysterious smoggy haze over the unusual planet's sunlight end. *Voyager 2* found that Uranus was full of surprises!

VOYAGER 2 took both these images of Uranus in 1986. The one on the left is in true color, as the human eye would see Uranus. Yellow and red were added to the picture on the right to highlight where smoggy haze gathers over the sunlit pole.

MANY MYSTERIOUS MOONS

Some of *Voyager 2*'s most amazing discoveries have to do with Uranus's moons. The spacecraft discovered ten small moons orbiting Uranus. This brought the 1986 total to 15 moons. And *Voyager 2* got the first close-up look at the five largest moons. Astronomers squinting through telescopes had long wondered about these moons.

FAR-OUT FACT

LITERATURE-LINKED MOONS

Most of our solar system's moons have names from ancient mythology. All of Uranus's 27 known moons are uniquely named after characters in plays by William Shakespeare and poems by Alexander Pope. Uranus's discoverer, William Herschel, found its two largest moons, Oberon and Titania, in 1787. William Lassell discovered Ariel and Umbriel in 1851. Almost a century later, in 1948, Gerard Kuiper spotted Miranda. These five moons were the only ones that had been found until a space probe visited in 1986. *Voyager 2* found ten more small moons: Juliet, Puck, Cordelia, Ophelia, Bianca, Desdemona, Portia, Rosalind, Cressida, and Belinda. (Twelve more moons have been discovered since then.)

VOYAGER 2 took these images of Uranus's two largest moons on January 24, 1986. Oberon (at left) has a tall mountain on its lower left edge. Titania (at right) has deep canyons along its right side.

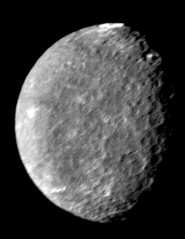

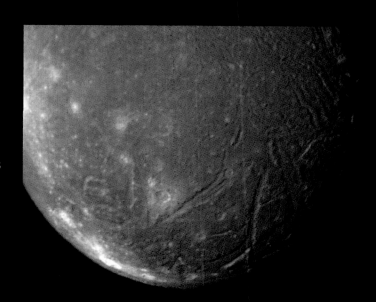

UMBRIEL (above) is Uranus's darkest moon. Ariel (right) has deep, long valleys that are easily seen in this *Voyager 2* image.

None of Uranus's moons are giants. Uranus's largest moon, Oberon, is only half the size of Earth's moon. Studying small faraway moons is difficult, even with powerful telescopes. So not much was known about Uranus's moons until *Voyager 2*. Would such wimpy worlds even be very interesting? Astronomers were not disappointed when *Voyager 2*'s close-up photos came in.

Uranus's largest moons turned out to be amazingly peculiar. The photos showed canyons, cliffs, cracks, and craters. Oberon has a mountain 6 kilometers (4 miles) high, nearly the height of North America's highest peak, Mount McKinley. Titania is an icy world of canyons and huge cracks. Long, deep valleys stretch across Ariel. Umbriel is a crater-covered moon.

Oddest of all is Miranda. "[It] is all the strange places we've come across rolled into one," said Voyager scientist Larry Soderblom. The small moon has deep canyons and zigzagging ridges. There are dark wrinkly areas next to bright icy patches. "You have to compare it to bizarre bits and pieces of what we've seen throughout the solar system," Soderblom said. All this on a world only one-seventh the size of Earth's moon. How did Uranus's moons get such weird features? "Something cataclysmic happened to Uranus early in its history and we don't understand what that really was," said Soderblom. Unique Uranus has secrets yet to share.

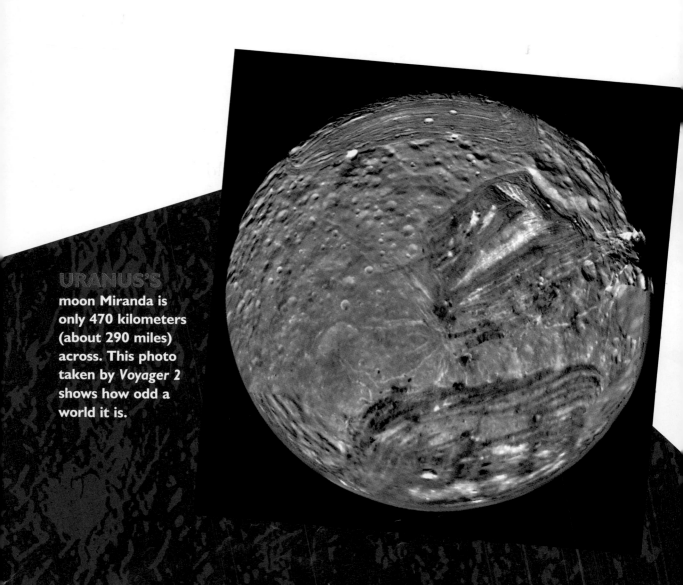

URANUS'S moon Miranda is only 470 kilometers (about 290 miles) across. This photo taken by *Voyager 2* shows how odd a world it is.

URANUS AT A GLANCE

Diameter: 51,118 kilometers (31,763 miles)

Volume: 63 Earths

Mass: 14½ Earths, or 86,849,000,000,000 trillion kilograms

Gravity: 75-pound kid would weigh 65 pounds

Position: Seventh planet from the Sun

Average Distance from Sun: 2,871 million kilometers
 (1,784 million miles)

Day Length: 17 hours, 14 minutes

Year Length: 30,687 Earth days (or about 84 Earth years)

Color: Pale blue

Atmosphere: 83% hydrogen; 15% helium, 2% methane

Surface: None

Temperature: −216° Celsius (−357° Fahrenheit)

Moons: 27

Rings: 13

Namesake: Greek god of the heavens and father of the Titans

Symbol:

URANUS

Planet Fast Facts

★ Uranus is the only one of our solar system's eight planets to be completely tilted over on its side. It spins like a bead on a string, not around like a top.

★ Sometimes one pole of Uranus faces directly toward the Sun while the other pole faces away.

★ Temperatures are about the same all over Uranus, even though some areas receive more sunlight.

★ Uranus only gets about 1/400th of the sunlight that Earth does.

★ Scientists think something the size of a planet might have knocked or pulled Uranus over onto its side.

★ It takes Uranus 84 Earth years to travel once around the Sun.

★ Spring, summer, autumn, and fall each last twenty-one years on Uranus.

★ William Herschel used a telescope to track Uranus and discovered it was a planet in 1781.

★ Uranus can be seen in the night sky, but it looks like a faint star.

★ Uranus is the third largest planet in the solar system after Jupiter and Saturn.

★ Uranus is a gas giant. It is a cold, windy, landless world made of gases and liquid.

★ Uranus is also called an ice giant, a type of large, cold, gaseous planet containing a lot of methane and ammonia.

★ Methane, or natural gas, gives Uranus its blue color.

* Beneath Uranus's cold atmosphere is a layer of liquid water, ammonia, and methane ice. The planet's core is probably solid rock.

* Uranus has the brightest clouds in the outer solar system—the solar system from Jupiter outward. They are created by warm methane that bubbles up to the surface from deep inside Uranus.

* Nine of Uranus's rings are thin, dense, and dark. They are made up of chunks of rock and ice. Four are fat, faint clouds of orbiting dust.

Uranus Moons Fast Facts

* Uranus has 27 known moons. There are likely more tiny ones still undiscovered.

* The five largest moons of Uranus are Titania, Oberon, Umbriel, Ariel, and Miranda. They range from 475 to 1,580 kilometers (295 to 982 miles) in diameter.

* Uranus's five biggest moons are worlds of ice and rock.

* Voyager 2 found ten small moons in 1986: Juliet, Puck, Cordelia, Ophelia, Bianca, Desdemona, Portia, Rosalind, Cressida, and Belinda.

* In 1999, an overlooked moon named Perdita was discovered in the Voyager 2 photographs.

* Telescopes on Earth discovered moons Caliban, Sycorax, Stephano, Setebos, Prospero, Francisco, Ferdinand, Margaret, and Trinculo between 1997 and 2003. Mab and Cupid were found with the Hubble Space Telescope in 2003.

Uranus Mission Fast Facts

★ No astronauts have traveled to Uranus, only a single robotic space probe, *Voyager 2*.

★ Spaceships will never land on Uranus. There is no land.

★ It took *Voyager 2* nearly 8½ years to reach Uranus. It launched in 1977 and arrived in 1986.

★ *Voyager 2* made its closest pass by Uranus for six hours on January 24, 1986.

★ The eleven instruments onboard *Voyager 2* studied Uranus's magnetic field, atmosphere, and weather, and measured its day to be 17.24 hours.

★ *Voyager 2* showed a surprising first close-up look at Uranus's five big moons.

★ While arriving at Uranus, *Voyager 2* discovered ten new moons and photographed nine of its rings.

Uranus Timeline of Exploration and Discovery

1781 William Herschel discovers Uranus using his telescope.

1787 William Herschel discovers moons Titania and Oberon.

1851 William Lassell discovers moons Ariel and Umbriel.

1948 Gerard Kuiper discovers moon Miranda.

1977 Astronomers on Earth discover Uranus's rings.

1986 *Voyager 2*, launched in 1977, becomes the first spacecraft to visit Uranus. It sends back almost 8,000 images of the planet and its dark ring system, and it discovers ten new moons.

1990s *Hubble Space Telescope*, launched in 1990, observes the planet's atmosphere, clouds, and changing seasons.

1997–2001 Astronomers discover nine more small moons using ground-based telescopes.

1999 Astronomers studying *Voyager 2* photographs find yet another moon.

TIMELINE
★

2003 *Hubble Space Telescope* discovers two more small moons.

2005 *Hubble Space Telescope* discovers two more rings.

2007–2008 Astronomers study Uranus's rings, edge-on, during its equinox.

SPACE shuttle *Discovery* carried the *Hubble Space Telescope* into orbit around Earth in 1990.

CHAPTER 2

A TELESCOPIC VIEW

Voyager 2 stacked up discoveries as it flew by Uranus in 1986. But it was a short visit. At its closest pass, *Voyager 2* was at Uranus for just six hours. The space probe closely observed about one third of a single day on Uranus. *Voyager 2*'s photos showed a solid blue sphere. It looked like a hazy giant gumball in space. Uranus had no colorful bands like Jupiter. There were no swirling storms like on Saturn. Scientists studying the images wondered: Is Uranus's weather and atmosphere always so boring? Or did *Voyager 2* just catch it on a calm day? With no more space probes on the way, astronomers had to turn to telescopes for answers.

FAR-OUT FACT

HUBBLE SPACE TELESCOPE

The *Hubble Space Telescope* is a powerful telescope and an orbiting spacecraft. Why send a bus-sized telescope into space? To get above Earth's messy atmosphere. Looking through air blurs a ground-based telescope's view. The *Hubble* orbits about 610 kilometers (380 miles) above our planet. Up there the view is much clearer. Space shuttle astronauts have repaired and upgraded *Hubble* over the years. Their efforts should keep the space telescope working until at least 2014.

ZOOMING IN ON URANUS

Luckily, as *Voyager 2* zipped past Uranus, a new kind of telescope was being built. In the 1990s the *Hubble Space Telescope* started giving us the next good look at the seventh planet. The *Hubble* proved that Uranus was not dull after all! In fact, the *Hubble* measured Uranus's clouds as the brightest among the solar system's gas giants. Uranus was suddenly a world with bands of zooming clouds

THIS 1998 *Hubble* image of Uranus uses colors to highlight the planet's bright clouds. (Watch a *Hubble* movie of Uranus's changing seasons at the Web site on page 47.)

THIS 2006 *Hubble* image of Uranus shows a storm, called a dark spot. The storm outlined by the white square is two-thirds the size of the United States.

FAR-OUT FACT

SHEPHERD MOON

There is a reason planets with rings often also have many small moons. The miniature moons sometimes help create rings. They are called shepherd moons because they keep the rings from wandering off. How? Shepherd moons orbit at the edges of the rings. A shepherd moon's gravity keeps the ring's dust, rock, and ice from drifting off into space. Shepherds Cordelia and Ophelia are the two moons closest to Uranus. In between their orbits is the Epsilon ring they shepherd.

and storms half the size of the United States. What was stirring up Uranus's atmosphere? Springtime! The seventh planet was finally coming out of its 21-year-long winter.

Uranus's stormy weather and blindingly bright clouds were not all that the *Hubble* saw. In 2003, the *Hubble* discovered two more tiny moons. Ground-based telescopes had also revealed other moons. By 2003, Uranus's moon total had reached 27. The *Hubble* also discovered two more rings in 2005.

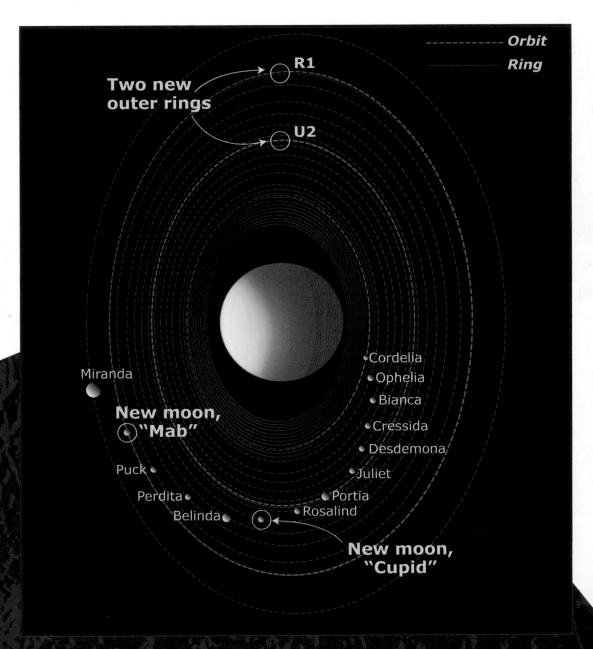

Orbit
Ring

R1

**Two new
outer rings**

U2

Miranda

**New moon,
"Mab"**

Puck

Perdita

Belinda

Cordelia
Ophelia
Bianca
Cressida
Desdemona
Juliet
Portia
Rosalind

**New moon,
"Cupid"**

HUBBLE Space Telescope
discovered a new pair of rings around
Uranus and two new small moons.

FAR-OUT FACT

SURPRISING DISCOVERY

Uranus's rings were discovered by accident. In 1977, astronomers watched as Uranus passed in front of a star. Observing a planet backlit by bright starlight is a good way to study its atmosphere. Astronomers ended up seeing something extra! They discovered nine rings circling Uranus. These were the first rings discovered around a planet other than Saturn. Now we know that all the gas giants have rings of some kind.

VOYAGER 2 took this picture of Uranus's rings in 1986. What looks like rain is actually bits of dust and other particles that move between rings.

AN EDGY LOOK

Season changes on Uranus offer more than wild weather. The start of autumn and spring creates a unique view of Uranus's rings. The start of these seasons is called an equinox. (It is called this on Earth, too.) An equinox happens as the Sun passes directly above the planet's equator. Uranus's equinox makes the rings appear on edge when viewed from Earth. It is like holding a CD flat between your fingers at eye level. You only see the thin edge, not much of the disc. This odd edge-on angle gives astronomers a unique view of Uranus's rings. The nine darker, denser, skinny rings fade into the darkness. And the clouds of dust that make up Uranus's four fat, faint rings suddenly show up clearly.

In 2007, astronomers around the world watched Uranus's equinox. It was a history-making event. The last equinox on Uranus was in the 1960s. No one even knew Uranus had rings back then. "We're seeing the rings edge-on for the first time since they were discovered in 1977," said an excited Mark Showalter. The astronomer

URANUS orbits tilted over on its side, so its rings wrap around the planet from top to bottom, like circles around a target. Earth's view of Uranus's rings changes as the seventh planet orbits the Sun—from edge-on to full circle.

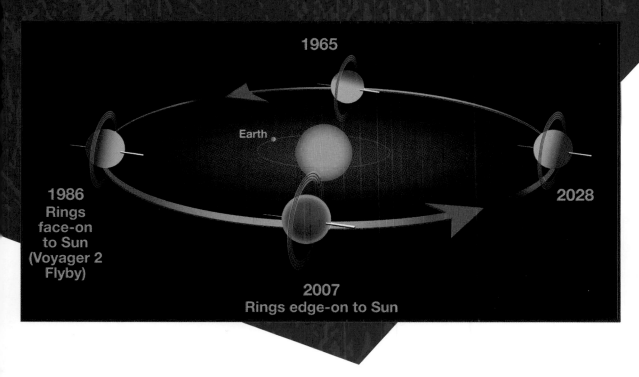

1965

Earth

1986
Rings
face-on
to Sun
(Voyager 2
Flyby)

2028

2007
Rings edge-on to Sun

was on the *Hubble Space Telescope* team that discovered two of these faint rings around Uranus in 2003.

RINGS ARE NOT FOREVER

Showalter is used to seeing new things. He discovered Uranus's moons Mab and Cupid. And as a scuba diver he has explored underwater worlds from Alaska to Australia. But even Showalter was amazed at what the equinox revealed.

Uranus's rings are changing—and fast! "There is a ring that wasn't there twenty years ago and there is an old ring that is gone," he said. *Voyager 2* photographed Uranus's rings back in 1986, including an inner ring called Zeta. But Zeta is now gone, and a new ring has appeared several thousand kilometers farther out

2003

2005

2007

THESE Hubble images show how Uranus's rings move from a straight-on view toward being on edge at equinox in 2007.

from the planet. So Uranus still has thirteen rings—just not the same thirteen rings it had a couple of decades ago.

"We used to think that even these faint dust rings would still take thousands or millions of years to evolve and change," said Showalter. Now scientists know a planet's rings can quickly change. Where could a new ring have come from? A house-sized rock from another ring "could have been bashed to smithereens," said Showalter. The cloud of dust created would spread around Uranus, forming a faint ring—at least for a while. All planetary rings come and go. Even the glorious rings of Saturn will disappear someday. "If humans had come along a hundred million years earlier or later, we might have missed the rings of Uranus or Saturn," said Showalter. "Rings are not forever, so enjoy them while you can."

CHAPTER 3

WHAT'S NEXT FOR URANUS?

THE W. M. Keck Observatory is on top of Mauna Kea, a mountain high enough to have snow even in Hawaii.

38

Astronomers will keep focusing their telescopes on Uranus in coming years. For now, it is their only option! No new space probes are on their way to Uranus. None are being planned, either. The *Hubble Space Telescope* will probably get a last glimpse or two of Uranus before the telescope stops working. After that, any big discoveries about the seventh planet will come from telescopes on Earth.

HAWAIIAN DELIGHT

Hawaii's Mauna Kea mountain is 4,200 meters (13,800 feet) tall. The thin, calm, dry air makes it a perfect site for the W. M. Keck Observatory. Each of the observatory's twin telescopes stands eight stories tall and weighs 300 tons. They are some of the world's largest and most sophisticated telescopes. Inside each is a mirror 10 meters (30 feet) across made up of 36 pieces perfectly fitted together. Both telescopes have view-sharpening adaptive optics. The Keck telescopes have taken the best ground-based telescope pictures of Uranus yet. They have studied its changing rings and seasons.

Ground-based telescopes are getting better at seeing through our soupy atmosphere. The best ones are built on mountaintops. Up there the thinner mountain air is less blurring. New telescope technology is also sharpening the view. Adaptive optics is the biggest advance. Special flexible mirrors, or optics, are placed inside the telescope.

These change shape, or adapt, to lessen blurring caused by moving air. A powerful computer constantly measures the blurring. It then changes the mirrors' shapes. The best ground-based telescope views of Uranus come from telescopes fitted with adaptive optics.

Scientists hope that better telescopes will help solve some of Uranus's many remaining mysteries, like its on again–off again stormy weather. Will it change with the next season? Even the idea that a giant collision caused

FAR-OUT FACT

WANT TO SEE URANUS?

Uranus can just barely be seen with the naked eye in a very dark night sky. But no one knew that Uranus was a planet until William Herschel tracked it using his telescope in 1781. If you manage to find Uranus in the night sky, it will look like a faraway star. With very good binoculars or a backyard telescope, Uranus looks like a pale blue disk. The planet-watching Web sites on page 47 can help you locate Uranus.

USING adaptive optics on the Keck telescope, astronomers took this sharp image of Uranus in 2004. The image recorded the planet in infrared light, which makes the rings appear red and highlights clouds.

WHAT'S NEXT FOR URANUS?

★

Uranus's famous sideways tilt is just a guess. Did something huge actually crash into it, or did the big invader's gravity just pull Uranus over during a close pass? And if something did knock Uranus over, what was it exactly—and where did it go? Answers to these questions would give us even more reason to be amazed by Uranus. It is a unique and fascinating world.

Words to Know

adaptive optics—Telescope technology that lessens the blurring effects of light traveling through the atmosphere.

astronomer—A scientist who studies moons, planets, stars, and the universe.

atmosphere—The gases that are held by gravity around a planet, moon, star, or other object in space.

comet—A large chunk of frozen gases, ice, and dust that orbits the Sun.

core—The center, usually solid, of a planet or moon.

craters—Bowl-shaped holes made by impact explosions on the surface of a planet or moon, often from comet or asteroid crashes.

day—The time it takes an object in space to complete one turn or spin.

equinox—The two times during a year when the Sun appears overhead at the equator and day and night are equal in length.

gas giant—A planet made of mostly gas and liquid with no land, such as Jupiter, Saturn, Uranus, and Neptune.

gravity—An attractive force on one object from another.

ground-based telescope—A telescope on Earth.

ice giant—A gas giant with large amounts of ammonia, methane, and water, such as Uranus and Neptune.

interstellar space—Space between the stars and not within a solar system.

magnetic field—The area of magnetic influence around a magnet, electric current, or planet.

WORDS TO KNOW
★

mass—The amount of matter in something.

methane—Natural gas, or a gas made of a combination of carbon and hydrogen.

moon—An object in space that naturally orbits a planet.

NASA—The National Aeronautics and Space Administration, the space agency of the United States.

nebulae—Clouds of dust and gas out in space, or cloudlike clusters of stars.

orbit—The path followed by a planet, moon, or other object around another object in space; to move around an object in space.

planet—A large, sphere-shaped object in space that orbits around a sun.

pole—One of two points on a sphere farthest from the equator; or either end of a magnet.

shepherd moon—A moon that orbits near a ring's edge and whose gravity keeps ring particles from escaping.

solar system—A sun and everything that orbits it.

space probe—A robotic spacecraft launched into space to collect information.

star—A large ball-shaped object in space made of gases that shines by its own light.

sun—The star in the center of a solar system.

volume—The amount of space something fills.

year—The time it takes for an object in space to travel around the Sun.

Find Out More and Get Updates

Books

Carruthers, Margaret. *The Hubble Space Telescope.* New York: Franklin Watts, 2003.

Carson, Mary Kay. *Exploring the Solar System: A History with 22 Activities.* Chicago: Chicago Review Press, 2008.

Fraknoi, Andrew. *Disney's Wonderful World of Space.* New York: Disney Publishing, 2007.

Landau, Elaine. *Uranus.* New York: Children's Press, 2008.

Miller, Ron. *Uranus and Neptune.* Brookfield, Conn.: Twenty-First Century Books, 2003.

Tocci, Salvatore. *A Look at Uranus.* New York: Franklin Watts, 2003.

FIND OUT MORE AND GET UPDATES
★

Solar System Web Sites

Solar System Exploration
  http://solarsystem.nasa.gov/kids

Uranus's Moons
  http://www.kidsastronomy.com/uranus/moons.htm

Uranus Exploration Web Sites

The Hubble Space Telescope
  http://hubblesite.org

The Voyager Missions
  http://voyager.jpl.nasa.gov

Uranus Movie

Watch Uranus's seasons change in this two-minute movie made from Hubble images. http://hubblesite.org/newscenter/archive/releases/1999/11/video/b/

Planet-watching Web Sites

NightSky Sky Calendar
  http://www.space.com/spacewatch/sky_calendar.html

StarDate Online: Solar System Guide
  http://stardate.org/resources/ssguide/uranus.html

Index

A

adaptive optics,
40–41
Ariel, 18
astronomy, 6

C

comet, 5, 6
Cupid, 35

H

Herschel, Caroline, 6
Herschel, John F. W.,
6
Herschel, William, 5,
6, 7, 16, 41
Hubble Space Telescope,
28, 31, 35, 39

J

Jupiter, 5, 7, 9, 27

K

King George III, 7
Kuiper, Gerard, 16

L

Lassell, William, 16

M

Mab, 35
Mars, 5

Mercury, 5
Miranda, 18

N

NASA, 10
Neptune, 7, 11

O

Oberon, 18

S

Saturn, 5, 7, 9, 10, 12,
27, 33, 37
Showalter, Mark,
34–37
Soderblom, Larry,
18–19
Stone, Ed, 13–14

T

telescopes, 16, 18, 27,
28, 31, 39–41
Titania, 18

U

Umbriel, 18
Uranus
atmosphere, 27, 31,
33
composition, 7
day, 12

discovery, 5, 6, 7
equinox, 34–35
moons, 16, 18–19,
31, 35
name, 7
rings, 31, 32, 33,
34–37
spin, 7–8, 12, 14
temperature, 14
tilt, 7, 41, 43
weather, 14–15, 27,
28, 31, 34, 41

V

Venus, 5
Voyager 1, 9, 11
Voyager 2, 9, 10, 11,
12, 13–16, 18, 27,
28, 36

W

W. M. Keck
Observatory, 40

Z

Zeta, 36